Poetry Set Free

Clare Campbell

chipmunkapublishing
the mental health publisher

Clare Campbell

All rights reserved, no part of this publication may be reproduced by any means, electronic, mechanical photocopying, documentary, film or in any other format without prior written permission of the publisher.

>Published by
>Chipmunkapublishing
>United Kingdom

http://www.chipmunkapublishing.com

Copyright © Clare Campbell 2018

ISBN   978-1-78382-410-6

Poetry Set Free

For my Mum and Dad who showed me how to believe in myself.

Clare Campbell

The Oak

Stepping out into the warm air
Immediately surrounded by trees
Green and purple, different shades
Bright against the grey sky

Wandering up the avenue of trees
Speaking vibrant life into an undecided atmosphere
Ahead is a rabbit, sensing our presence it runs,
white tail flicking a warning to potential predators

Standing still an old Oak draws attention
Proud and tall against the skyline
Victor over sun, wind, rain and snow
It leaves a sense of peacefulness and calm

Clare Campbell

Open Horizons

Step by step, one foot after the other
The breeze flowing through my hair
And caressing any exposed skin
I walk into freedom, beauty all around

Temporary though it is
It is valuable like a hug
Embraced by the great outdoors
Horizons broadened by the open sky

Eyes wide open, taking in delicate shades
My ears are gently invaded by birdsong
A deep breath of fresh air reveals a pure smell
My hungry senses are filled and satisfied

Truth Versus Lies

Simple truths mock complex lies
The truth has a substance,
A groundedness that lies can only imitate
The imitation lightweight for all its solid appearance

Each time the truth is told
It rings true no matter what
Even rare outlandish statements have weight
They speak confidently and stand tall

Clare Campbell

A Soul's Journey

Starting at the beginning
Who knows when the bundle of cells
Gains its most precious part?
Its own unique eternal soul

Whether arriving at the moment of viability
Or in the breath that precedes the first cry
The soul is precious, deep inside
Yet always present- behind every thought

Early experiences shape the vulnerable soul
For better or worse it takes shape
Growing in strength and, if blessed, beauty
The soul travels on and becomes more sturdy

Now the soul shapes life
As life shapes the soul
Some, barely aware, keep it imprisoned
Others treasure and nurture it

Through great achievements and crippling grief
The soul marches on like a well trained soldier
Holding the whole person's internal world
Keeping it together through thick and thin

As the end draws near
The soul begins its preparations
Leaving behind its grateful host
Freed at last, the soul journeys on

Poetry Set Free

The Importance of Motherhood

Often beginning in uncertainty
Sometimes long hoped for
Sometimes precipitating complete surprise

Growing mysteriously in the dark
A bundle of cells slowly transforming
Hour by hour, day by day

At once too long and too short
Molecule upon molecule taking their own time to form
Twelve weeks brings the unknown into sharp reality

Thirty eight weeks soon arrives
Pain brings forth precious, unique beauty
Though tiny and weak the baby exudes strength

Sleepless nights elongate the days
But soon crawling, quickly walking
Talking follows too

Dedication and deep seated primal love
Permit, encourage and lead
That tiny baby into toddlerhood

Years flash by and by
Clothes and shoes fit for moments not months
Traits and personality emerge, individuality shines through

Then all too soon, a bittersweet goodbye
All grown up with a life of their own, Baby leaves,

Clare Campbell

Leaving the certainty that Motherhood is the noblest calling of all

Gentle Guardian

Gentle guardian without knowing it
Some weeks pass while the mysteries of life begin
Always an element of surprise
For most delight with threads of trepidation settles in

The remaining time is for preparation
Though life carries on while new life grows
Changes begin inside and out,
Already taking care of the unborn child

Pain heralds the new arrival
Joy and contentment wrap around the little bundle
Unimaginable, unimagined love overflows
And informs all the hard work that follows

A mother's love cannot be compared with any other
Covering growing pains, growing pains and more
The bond, once physical, can never be broken
Privileged to be the recipient, the child returns the special love.

Clare Campbell

Presence

Present in the darkest night
Present in long moments waiting for the light
Present when I feel alone
Present when all I want is to go home

Present when the distance seems far
Present in the closest times
Present when distress wreaks calm
Present when all I can see is darkness

Present when contentment reigns
Present in the joy and peace
Present in the deepest pain
Presence that will call me home one day

Grace and Glory

Close your eyes tight
And see a bright light
Warm but not dazzling
Glowing and imbued with life

As your new sight adjusts
See shapes begin to form
Row upon row of angels
Wings and halos adorning each one

Then in the centre
The object of worship
Father Son and Holy Spirit
All attention focused on them

Glorious in their majesty
Words cannot describe the scene
Overwhelming awe draws all to their knees
Lost in wonder and praise

Yet among the glory is humanity
Jesus was born as a tiny baby
The birth a miracle
As a man a miracle maker

Saving and serving those around him
Constantly communicating with his Father
Taking obedience and strength from Gethsemane
Jesus went willingly to the cross

Unthinkable suffering, a criminal's death
Unimaginable pain at separation from heaven
Rising victorious, no greater miracle
Sin, death and hell conquered forever

The way was paved for salvation
Relationships formed of love and grace
Imagine being fully known and fully forgiven
Imagine love as solid as a rock, a place of safety

Imagine a friend who listens all the time
Imagine a Saviour who picks you up when you fall
All this is ours through the Holy Spirit
And the greatest sacrifice- the Father giving his Son

The Transaction

Into the night
The man disappears
Black clothing head to foot
And a moonless night
Allow him to be almost invisible

Cutbacks mean no streetlights
Not in this part of town
The location for the man's business.
It's wrong and risky
But the gamble pays large dividends

Waiting no less than a minute
The customer turns up
Similarly dressed except for a silver chain
The transaction is quick and efficient
Both leave satisfied, and as though they were never ever there.

Clare Campbell

Entering the Profession

The decision was made three years ago
And many events, good and bad, are past
And much hard work has developed the necessary skills

Finally, all the boxes ticked, all paperwork done
Now with a simple payment the PIN is mine
Everything has changed because of a number

No more student life, someone else's responsibility.
Standing tall on the outside
Quaking with fear on the inside

Each new step leaves a footprint
Assessed by colleagues and therefore nerve-wracking
But time and support build confidence

Long days, earlys, lates, time passes quickly
What was daunting becomes dull, but one day it sinks in
I'm doing what I trained for- making a difference

Precious One

You can't be with me 24/7
But even when you're far, you're near
You're inside my heart

Your work takes you far
Exotic locations your second home
But you're inside my heart

The times when you're away
Test my resilience
Still you're inside my heart

The day you return
I hold you in my arms
The sun shines within my heart

Clare Campbell

Aquarium

Large and rectangular
Sitting where it's easily viewed
It's eye catching and beautiful

The gravel is multicoloured
The goldfish stand out against it
They swim lazily around the green plants

The world of fish is simple
Swimming then resting
Noticing vibrations as viewers draw near

There is, though a constant search for food
Keeping a tiny mind occupied
But only satisfied once a day

The ceremonial dropping of the food
Leads to frantic activity
Bobbing up to the surface again and again

The fish now look so animated
They soon decimate the delicate flakes
Contentment reigns and all is peaceful once again

Watching the fish is mesmerising
Their bright colours pleasing to the eye
Watching random movements leads to a sense of calm.

Burgeoning Life

The seed is tiny
It is insignificant
And as light as a feather

It sits precariously on my finger
The flowerpot and soil are prepared
I gently imbed the seed in the soil

It's wrapped warmly in its soil cocoon
Unpromising to look at,
It rests as though dead

Weeks pass, water is given
Then the first sign of life
A peeping green shoot

It provides welcome contrast against brown soil
So small and delicate
It still looks insignificant

Dribbles of water feed the bud
It gradually rises above the soil
Taking its time, the feeble stalk grows

Little by little, bit by bit
Inch by inch it grows
Now it looks as though it can hold its own

Clare Campbell

Repotting is necessary
As more space is needed
Finally the seed is showing promise

Happy in its new home
The Sunflower bursts into life
Bringing a smile to the faces of all who see it

Somehow in the magic of nature
The Sunflower is true to its name
And follows the sun on its journey through the sky

Waiting for my Love

Your natural beauty shines through
The endearing efficiency of the work that carries you away
Means my face lights up when I finally see you
Reflecting the glow that attracts me to you

The time we spend together
Brightens up my life
I would be lost without you
You add mysterious value to my soul

Your eyes sparkle like crystal
Your smile is a treat I wait for
My love for you is unwavering, always
Counting the seconds until I can hold you in my arms

Clare Campbell

The Challenge

Trees are dancing in the wind
Storm rain providing the rhythm
Dusk is falling, lights are coming on,
Droplets become little containers of light

As the puddles form
They define the low places
And wait for the unwary,
So they can wash their feet

The storm hesitates in one place
Hovering, the picture of innocence
But wanting to do itself justice
Soaking as many as it can

A Bibliophile's Perfect Day

First is the cover
Designed to be eye catching
But gives no real clue
About the quality of the words
Held tightly on its pages

Then the decision to lift it up
Feel the weight of it
Satisfying in your hand
And the new book smell
Drifts from nose to brain

The smell is enticing
And initiates the turning of the book
To see whether the back cover
Fulfils the promise of the front
The words printed there pique interest

Standing in the queue to pay
It's impossible not to start,
The first page draws you in
So it's frustrating having to stop
And hand over cash for the book

Today is a rare day off
No commitments, phone on silent
So next stop is Costa
And of the myriad varieties
You select a simple but tasty Americano

Finding a corner seat
You settle in and begin to read

Clare Campbell

The pages turn themselves, the plot thickens,
Drama unfolding, wrapped deep within the characters' world,
The delicious coffee gradually goes cold.
The Entity

Each tiny sound ricochets around the room
Empty now it boasts the ghosts of what went before
The cacophony fills the ears of nobody
It is alive but with no real form

Sweeping through the silent dust
The Entity has its own way
Ruling over a non-existent Kingdom
The formless one wields its power

Light and Life

Two halves yet they don't make a whole
Instead there is a yawning chasm of darkness
It threatens to engulf the life filled part
That fights a losing battle

The battle will, though, ultimately be victorious
Darkness has already been defeated
Defeated by glorious unique unquenchable light
Defeated by the Creator who gives light

The Creator made all things
And when darkness threatened ultimate destruction
Redeemed all creation forever
With the most precious life of all

Clare Campbell

Fickle Fans

Long awaited by most
Then welcomed and wished away in equal measure
Warm days enhanced by the smell of freshly mown grass
A time of leisure and relaxation

Long days end in starry beauty
Weekends swept away under the spell of sports
Playgrounds filled with bundles of energetic laughter
Summer brings joy mitigated by humid lack of sleep
Thunderstorms bring spectacle and relief.

Mysterious Fiery Mass

Constantly on duty
Never ever at rest
Sometimes seeming to disappear
But simply fulfilling duties elsewhere

Unfathomable in its majesty
Though so far outstripped by its Creator
A fiery mass, its power unforgiving
Though it brings gentle warmth

Hidden away by dark clouds
It seems that rain can wash away its power
But, when it breaks through, creating a rainbow
The world admits its magnificence

Clare Campbell

The Forest

A vast ocean of green
Pleases the eye with its different shades
Inviting the viewer to wander among the trees

Any walker that accepts the invitation
Must take each step humbly
Walking as though in a sacred place

The forest has a life and character of its own
Its life force is tangible on entry
There is a hierarchy among the trees

This hierarchy is precious and firm
Each species knows and accepts its place
At the heart, Queen of them all, the Oak.

Background Beauty

As the day draws to a close
The sky gradually turns from blue to black
But there is a stage in between
The moments of background beauty

The gathering darkness and light pollution
Turn the sky a deep purple
But this is a big city
The commute means focus is on heading home

Unnoticed the purples decorates the sky
Before succumbing to the blackness of night
Helped by the switching out of the office lights
Which makes the late workers stand out

The remaining lights reflecting off the river
Makes a rainbow of sorts
Turning a workaholic environment
Into a beautiful scene

Clare Campbell

Little Ferry

Sparkling water greets the hull
The boat slips through the water
Waves gently break creating a little white water

Rocking gently over the muted swell
Faithfully carrying its seaworthy passengers
The destination? A sun-kissed Island

Arriving at the jetty, disembarkment ensues
Eagerly but not too briskly
The holiday feeling has already set in

Nature's Friendly Greeting

Early, before the dawn
The world is still sleeping
But the sky is an expectant grey
Waiting for the pinks and oranges that herald the new day

As the bright pastels filter across the canopy
Early risers somehow know it is time to wake
Opening the curtains they are treated to an artist's picture
Starting the day with that image imperceptibly lifts their mood

Sitting in traffic they choose not to honk the horn
Instead marvelling at the changing skies
Arriving at work their smile is mirrored by colleagues
The day proceeds, all influenced by the beautiful dawn.

Clare Campbell

Winter

Different people respond differently
There is a wide range of reactions
Some welcome it like an old friend
Others try to hide from it

Crispy, biting, intense, freezing,
Wind chill, frost, simply chilly
Different ways cold is experienced

Thermal layers, hats, gloves,
Scarves, thick woollen socks;
Different ways of combatting the cold

But there's nothing quite like a long walk,
Frost on the ground, and returning, having fought
To centrally heated warmth and a well-brewed cup of tea.

Man versus Nature

In its original state, perfect
And so diverse
Every aspect of creation beautiful

Different continents with unique pleasures
Sparkling snow contrasts with windswept barren deserts
Oceans competing for attention against trees of many shades

But a tiny part of this creation
Marches across continents, an invading force
Tearing down trees, wrecking landscapes for hidden treasure

Naturally passive, there is no defence
The destructive army lays waste to beauty
Nature turned against itself, unnatural warmth decimating habitats.

Clare Campbell

My son

When I first held you
My hands around your tiny frame
I knew I would always love you

As you grew and grew
Fed bountifully by your doting mother
I knew I would always love you

The times when you cried and cried
Refused to be comforted by my cradling arms
Still I knew I would always love you

At school age you sometimes ran wild
And wore my patience paper thin
But I knew I would always love you

When you were grown and ready to leave
Off to make your own way in the world, you turned
And I knew I'd be ok because I would always love you

Eternal Love

No words can begin to describe
Nothing can ever compare
Completely outside our comprehension
And yet made known by mercy

First an unimaginably complete relationship
Suddenly, earth-shatteringly split apart
Though grace ensured contact remained
Spoken through beauty then fire and cloud

Individuals guided the people
Only through the inspiration of the constant Presence
A stormy chequered relationship
Marked by mercy and forgiveness

Then in the most humble circumstances
Eternal unfathomable love is expressed
Unremarkable to most, the greatest miracle is quietly worked
A tiny baby visited by shepherds and Kings

Loved and nurtured by his mother
And both his heavenly and earthly father
Surprising his parents by naturally staying long in his Father's House
But faithfully learning his trade until the right time

Blessed at baptism with his Father's unshakable approval
Blessing and challenging those he met
Transforming individual lives

Clare Campbell

Redeeming the whole world through unthinkable sacrifice

Gone for a time, scarring heaven
The Son of God ended the last enemy
Glorious in resurrection, disbelief displaced by joy
The Holy One had vanquished sin and death

Teaching still for a time then returning to his rightful place
Completing heaven for eternity
Causing great rejoicing among the angels
Earth was not bereft, the Comforter was given

A gift of indescribable grace
He makes the way for new life,
For hope and joy and peace;
Father, Son and Holy Spirit lavish life giving love on us.

Animal Companions

Domesticated from wild roots
Cats will never admit that they're owned
Stalking through house, garden and streets,
Their territory marked out and defended

By contrast dogs are faithful servants
Eyes communicating content obedience
Wagging tails confirming enjoyment of close relationship

Both give and receive affection
But only to their human guardians
Cat meeting dog results in a melee
Fur flies, howls and growls rend the air

Clare Campbell

Carnival!

Street upon street is closed, cordoned off
Traffic gridlocks and drivers hoot horns
But it's not an accident this time
Today it's Carnival!

People crowd the streets
Peering over each others' shoulders
Vying for position
A young lad is held high so he can see

Fair haired and blue eyed
His young brain struggles to process sights and sounds
Greens, blues, purples, oranges
Dancing pulls attention to the mass of movement

Sounds are filling the air
Ears are filled with a combination of lively music
And chanting and clapping
Overwhelming joy fills the crowd's hearts

Weathering the weather

Open your eyes
See the grey sky
See the storm brewing

Open your eyes
Prepare for the wind and rain
Batten down the hatches

Open your eyes
Blink as the raindrops fall
Wrap your coat around you

Open your eyes
Look for the sun
See the rainbow.

Clare Campbell

Rainbow

A well-brewed cup of tea
Brings a smile to my face
Driving through light traffic with my favourite song on
the radio
Brings a smile to my face
Arriving at work and seeing my favourite team
Brings a smile to my face
Having my break at just the right time
Brings a smile to my face
Coming home, greeting my precious children
Brings a smile to my face
Finally relaxing in front of the TV
Brings a smile to my face

Looking out of the window
I see grey clouds that have been raining all day
Out of nowhere the clouds part
The brilliant sun shines forth
A magnificent rainbow is formed, it
Brings a smile to my face
And I realise that sunshine is everywhere in my life.

King for a day?

Kings resplendent in their majesty
Hold court, respect paid to them
Making decisions with advice from courtiers
Ruling their Kingdoms with due ceremony

Keeping the inevitable factions under control
More talented than a seasoned juggler
Signing documents they've barely had time to read
Yet spotting errors and deceptions

Kings, royalty personified
Living lives steeped in riches
Their splendour, power and position
Jails them in guilded cages from birth to death.

Clare Campbell

Chapel

The light is the first indication
Adjusting gladly the pupils dilate
Compensating for the transition
No bright sunlight, instead it is muted, causing shadows

Next a deep breath betrays the change of atmosphere
The warm dusty air that is heavy and intriguing
Silence fills the ears and gently quiets the soul
A holy reverence fills the mind

Stepping onwards past monuments and pews
Dedicated to their service for hundreds of years
Sitting on wood that has seen many people
A long moment of absolute quiet prepares for what is to come

Filing in, imitating the Angels looking on
Having taken their places the traditional words begin
The perfect introduction to the long awaited anthem
First, though, the Organ begins to play, yet silence remains

Then the first notes, treble, countertenor, tenor and bass
Fill the whole chapel, ringing out and overwhelming the senses
'Jesu, joy of man's desiring' perfectly pitched
The pure sound flows into heart and soul

As the choral music concluded the sacred story
'Thou dost ever lead Thine own
In the love of joys unknown'
Those present are left close to tears and closer to their God.

Easter

A day of celebration
Death and hell finally broken
The way to heaven opened
Everyone freed and healed

A day of celebration
Angels in heaven rejoice
Father Son and Holy Spirit
United, three in one

A day of celebration
Eternity fixed forever
Perfection rules, not darkness
The Light could not be put out.

Clare Campbell

Barbecue

Long days and short nights
Alarm clocks made redundant by the dawn chorus
Waking too early to a stunning sky
Pinks and oranges decorate the world's ceiling

Having started too soon the day holds promise
The few clouds soon wander nonchalantly away
Now only the sun interrupts the pure blue
No doubt remains, it's perfect BBQ weather

The charcoal is satisfyingly primitive
Firelighters fulfil the cave man's need for flame
As soon as the correct heat is achieved
The marinaded food goes on the grill

Soon enticing smells fill the air
The smoke combined with the sauce
Before long steak and burgers are plated up
And the family enjoy a summer feast.

The flowers

Daisies form a daisy chain
A classic sign of summer
When days are long and blissful
And all is right with the world

Roses form a romantic gift
A classic sign of love
When days are long and blissful
And all is right with the world

Tulips form a sign of spring
A classic gift of beauty
When days are long and blissful
And all is right with the world

Conkers form a classic game
A sure sign of Autumn
When days are shorter but full of life
And all is right with the world

Holly forms a sign of winter
When frost writes patterns everywhere
When days are filled with the threat of snow
But all is right with the world.

Clare Campbell

Shy Nature

A flash of colour
Gone again, then returning
Enhanced by bright light from above
And eye catching flower beds below

The butterfly flaps its wings again
Then alights on a delicate rose petal
It spreads its wings to drink in the warmth
And displays its complex, pretty pattern

A quiet step to get a better view
Is enough to startle the shy insect
It swiftly flies away to safety
Leaving a trail of beautiful images.

Flying

Take each step as it comes
Look at where you're going
Check both ways before you cross the road
All sound advice, but sometimes you need to fly

Unfold your wings, take a deep breath
Look up at the pure blue sky
Jump up, flap your wings, then begin to soar
Everything is different when you're surrounded by air

Mighty oaks become dots of green
Towering blocks of flats become mundane squares,
Vast fields like a patchwork quilt
Swoop down to see the Lego people

Spread your wings, fly higher,
Now passing a plane, see the shocked faces,
Smile and wave like Royalty
Freedom tingles from scalp to toes.

Clare Campbell

Photograph

A sparkling drop of water
Dwarfed by its surroundings-
A long thin blade of grass.
For a time it shimmered in the sunlight
Before evaporating into nothing

Its brief moment to shine
Did not go unnoticed
An early rising photographer
Captured it in all its glory
Before it followed its destiny

The high definition image
Was developed with care
And placed on a canvass
As tall as a man;
That tiny drop now huge

That tiny drop, with pure light glinting off it
Now famous and attracting attention
Instead of being completely missed,
The transient and insignificant
Immortalised in print.

The Power of Water

As far as the eye can see
All around are shades of green
Quiet fills the atmosphere
The lute-like birdsong is muted

Bursting through the centre
Of this idyllic scene
Is the majestic waterfall
It sparkles in the sunlight

Stealing the viewer's gaze
The impressive rush of water
Streams over the dead rocks
Bringing them to life.

Clare Campbell

Autumn

Taking its time to fall
The leaf caresses the ground
Joining the patchwork
That is adorning the tarmac

Autumn transforms the park
Turning it upside down
Colour is low, not high;
The season marks out the dedicated

Those who are true park members
Stand firm through frost and ice
Walking faithfully along well worn paths
Always appreciating the varying beauty.

Mountain Top

The cool air refreshes the climbers
Now they can take their rest
Air is thinner here but breath comes more easily

Bathed in misty light
Achievement informs relaxation
Finally protests from tired muscles are heeded

Was it worth the toil?
There are no dwellings here
And so descent is inevitable

Questioning the value of ascent
The mountain top challenges its conquerors
Those who stay in the valley will never know the answer.

Clare Campbell

Wicked Weather

No two days precisely the same
Making predictions a complex though in exact science
Looked for and listened to as gospel truth
Discussed as part of a daily ritual

The day dawned quietly enough
Inclement weather building through the small hours
Waiting for people to brave the outdoors
Punishing them for the necessary commute

Light grey is swept away by dark grey
Confounding those hoping for the sun
Wind, whistling, whooping and whooshing
Unremitting, enjoying freedom though not causing absolute havoc.

Scene of Quiet Beauty

Golden fields as far as the eye can see
Bypassing the horizon they reach to the sky
Blue meets gold in bright duet
Light and life are the song they sing

Birds are drawn to the solitary tree
Seated in comfort they appreciate the quiet beauty
Rest is found here, predators are far away
Peaceful gentleness defines the whole scene.

Clare Campbell

Night time

Night time wanders across the sky
Lights come on, beacons in the gathering darkness
Guiding some home, lighting the way out for others

But each light is polluting
Scaring away the beauty of the night sky
Sometimes only the moon can be seen
Glorious, it reigns over a nearly invisible kingdom

Ruling, it has a responsibility
Showing the order of the days,
In a way the sun cannot
Though only reflected light, it has a life of its own.

Where I Want To Stay

The landscape is confused
Not knowing whether to be high or low
The contrast is awe inspiring
A spectrum of colour soothes the gap

Reflections double the picturesque scene
Water providing the perfect mirror
This is the place I want to stay
The place where stillness feeds contentment.

Clare Campbell

Jigsaw

The picture on the box is so inviting
But greeted by a muddle, the first task
Is sorting all the pieces

Gradually the edge pieces reveal themselves
Joining the frame together brings a sense of satisfaction
Now the real work begins

The pieces are deceptive
Looking as though they don't fit
When rotated they join perfectly

Each one has its place
Little by little they link up
Patience is rewarded by a box perfect picture.

Scrabble

Each letter taken one by one
Or in a small handful
The square letters somehow satisfying

Placing it on the board
Brings its own satisfaction
A long word doubly so

Soon the board begin to fill
Both simple and unusual words adorn it
Putting down letters becomes more difficult

Finally the green bag is empty
A sense of disappointment or relief
Points are added up and the winner is decided

Clare Campbell

The Walk

Light glistens off the water
The lake is crystal clear
And still, as though ice.
There is not a breath of wind

There is no wildlife
It is isolated and so quiet
The stillness is tangible
Creating a peaceful scene

A bench welcomes hikers
Those who have made the long trek
Mile after mile, anticipation growing
Today is sunny but not too warm

Sitting there, close enough to see their reflection
Inviting reflection on life and living
Seeing wonder and possibilities
Long miles were worth it; they've bought inspiration.

Near-perfect Moment

Walking briskly in the chilly wind
Pushchairs and wayward little ones
Cross my path, causing me to halt
Mothers, chatting, carry on, oblivious
But the cuteness of the little ones causes me to smile

Now dodging a cyclist I resume my walk
Anticipation delighting my inner thoughts
The piercing notes of a penny whistle
Interrupt my contemplations, informing me I'm passing a busker

Nearing my destination, the anticipation grows
Arriving, I push open the branded door
And welcome the blast of warm air
Heavily tinged with the aroma of coffee

Today the queue is short
My order is dealt with efficiently
And with a semi-genuine smile
A good book and a great coffee, a near-perfect moment.

Clare Campbell

The beautiful game

Eleven men working as a unit
Facing eleven men equally bound
Each with their hopes and dreams
Each talented and unique

The whistle blows, battle begins
Carefully taught strategies
Are lost in the heat of the moment
Passing forward, closing in, intercepted again

Frustration and new formation
Adrenaline causes greater speed
The forward flicks the ball across the box
The waiting striker receives; in a split second

He shoots! He scores!

A wave of cheering flows around the Arsenal fans
While the striker is bundled by his mates
Attempt after attempt is thwarted by both goalies
1-0 is enough, the 3 valuable points banked.

Time

Too short or too long
Going too quickly or too slowly
Sometimes we wish time away
Other times we want a moment to last forever

Time has existed since the beginning of the universe
It witnessed the creation of stars and planets
Unaffected it simply carried on its march forwards
Nothing can interfere with it

Time ticks away inexorably
A law unto itself
It cannot be tamed
Nothing can stand in its way

Time is measured, first by sun and moon
Then by clockwork with audible ticks
Now digital technology measures nanoseconds
Impossible to engage with, it owns us all.

Clare Campbell

Law Enforcement

Radio on low to break up the hours
Eventually the suspect is on the move
Blue jeans and purple hoodie
Automatically and immediately noted

Now good judgement is needed
Following the car, not too closely
But not letting it escape
It takes skill and precision

Driving too fast through city streets
Increases the danger of being noticed
But, heading for the industrial estate,
The risk definitely increases

Pulling up close to the target
The detective nonchalantly leaves his car
Walks briskly up to the criminal
The arrest is made before he knows he's there

Tate Modern

Gloriously unashamedly distinctive
It endows the skyline with something proudly unique
A fine piece of architecture,
The impressive millennium bridge draws devotees in

Once inside time and reality are suspended
Eyes and ears working like Trojans
Conscious and subconscious mind under siege
After the initial moments, choices can be made

Different rooms have diverse atmospheres
Each reaction unique and personal
Some exhibits win barely a glance
Others demand long contemplation

The outcome is calm enjoyment
A hunger for more but time has struck back
Having to leave prompts a promise to return
Memories feed and augment the hunger for more

Clare Campbell

The Television

Much researched and technically challenging
A revolution in the world of entertainment
Moving pictures to accompany the sound
Though flickering and black and white

Gathering round the small box
Disbelief soon gives way to enjoyment
Starting out the domain of a privileged few
Spreading like a contagious disease

Soon an integral part of every living room
A new wave takes over with Colour
Bursting on to the screens
Taking the viewers into the centre of the action

The evolution from those first small boxes
To huge plasma screens dominating the room
Meant sports and films became all encompassing
A cinematic experience in the comfort of the home

Poetry Set Free

This anthology has poems for almost any occasion. It flows freely and at times enchantingly, unfettered by the constraints of rhyme. There a poems that bring a new perspective to every day events, poems to make you smile, poems that will initiate thought and reflection and poems that will ignite in you the creative spark we are all blessed with. Some poems allow glimpses of the Author's personal and treasured Christian beliefs but the poems are all potential sources of enjoyment and inspiration for readers of all faiths and none.

www.ingramcontent.com/pod-product-compliance
Ingram Content Group UK Ltd.
Pitfield, Milton Keynes, MK11 3LW, UK
UKHW041301180426
11947UKWH00009B/610